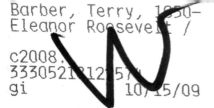

Eleanor Roosevelt

Terry Barber

ACTIVIST
SERIES

Eleanor Roosevelt is published by
Grass Roots Press, a division of Literacy Services of Canada Ltd.

PHONE 1–888–303–3213
WEBSITE www.grassrootsbooks.net

ACKNOWLEDGMENTS

We acknowledge the financial support of the Government of Canada through the Book Publishing Industry Development Program (BPIDP) for our publishing activities.

We acknowledge the support of
the Alberta Foundation for the Arts
for our publishing programs.

Editor: Dr. Pat Campbell
Image research: Dr. Pat Campbell
Book design: Lara Minja, Lime Design Inc.

Library and Archives Canada Cataloguing in Publication

Barber, Terry, date
    Eleanor Roosevelt / Terry Barber.

ISBN 978-1-894593-87-8

    1. Roosevelt, Eleanor, 1884-1962. 2. Presidents' spouses—United States—Biography. 3. Readers for new literates. I. Title.

PE1126.N43B36334 2008   428.6'2   C2008-901994-6

Printed in Canada

Contents

The white women sit together.

The First Lady Breaks the Law

It is 1939. People meet in a large room. The room is filled with black people and white people. Blacks sit with blacks. Whites sit with whites. Black people and white people cannot sit together. This is the law.

The meeting is in Birmingham, Alabama.

Eleanor sits with Mary McLeod Bethune.
January 13, 1939

The First Lady Breaks the Law

A tall white woman walks into the room. She breaks the law. She sits with the black people. Many people are shocked. The woman is the wife of the U.S. President. Her name is Eleanor Roosevelt.

Eleanor is the First Lady of the U.S. from 1933 to 1945.

The White House is the home of the U.S. President.

The White House

The First Lady Breaks the Law

Eleanor lives in the **White House**. Her world is filled with comfort. Her world is safe. Eleanor does not want a safe life. She wants to change the U.S. Eleanor wants to make the U.S. a better place.

Eleanor stands inside the White House.

Eleanor's
mother,
Anna Hall.

Eleanor in 1887.

Early Years

Eleanor is born in 1884. Her parents belong to **high society**. Her father is rich. Her mother is beautiful. Eleanor does not look like her mother. Eleanor is plain. She feels ugly. Eleanor thinks her mother does not like her.

Eleanor's mother tells Eleanor: "You have no looks. See to it that you have manners."

Eleanor and her father in 1889.

Early Years

Eleanor spends lots of time with her father. He teaches her to ride horses. He tells her stories. She is her father's pet. Eleanor feels loved when she is with him. Her father is the centre of her world.

Eleanor's father has a drinking problem.

Eleanor's father sits with his children.

Early Years

Eleanor's life changes when she is eight. Her mother gets sick and dies. Her father dies a year later. Eleanor and her brothers must live with their grandmother. She is very strict. Eleanor is sent to a girls' school in England.

Eleanor's father kills himself.

The girls' school in England.

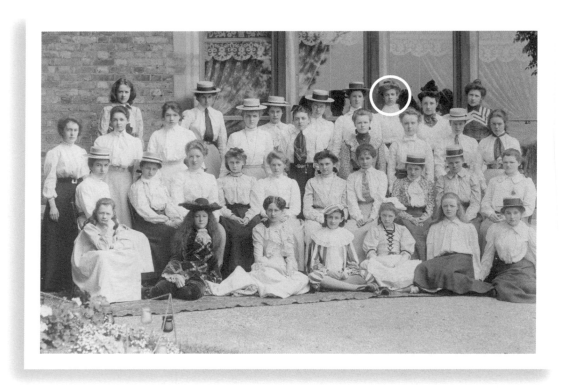

Eleanor and her classmates.

Early Years

It is 1899. Eleanor is excited. She is starting a new life. Eleanor is a good student. She is kind and helpful. The other students like Eleanor. She begins to like herself. Eleanor begins to believe in herself.

Eleanor moves to England at age 14.

Eleanor, age 14.

Eleanor's **coming-out** photo.
1902

Early Years

Eleanor returns to New York. She is 18. High society plans dances and parties for young women. They meet young men. They are expected to find husbands. Eleanor still questions her looks. She does not know that her inner beauty attracts others.

Young women meet young men from high society at a coming-out party.

Eleanor works with immigrants on this street.

Early Years

Eleanor goes to parties and dances for a year. But she wants more out of life. Eleanor begins to work in the **slums.** She works with **immigrants.** She teaches the children to dance. Most rich women will not even enter the slums.

Eleanor works for the Junior League.

Franklin Roosevelt in 1903.

Eleanor and Franklin

Eleanor feels good when she helps others. She also feels good because a young man wants to marry her. His name is Franklin Roosevelt. He knows Eleanor will help him. She will help him to make his dreams come true.

Franklin is Eleanor's fifth cousin.

The Roosevelt family in 1919.

Eleanor and Franklin

Eleanor and Franklin marry in 1905. They have six children. Eleanor is very busy with her family. She has maids and cooks to help her. In 1909, one of the Roosevelt's children dies. This loss stays with Eleanor all her life.

In 1910, Franklin wins an election. He becomes a New York senator.

Eleanor is not happy after Franklin's affair.
1920

Eleanor and Franklin

Eleanor suffers another loss. Franklin falls in love with another woman. Eleanor offers to divorce Franklin. A divorce would end his political career. Eleanor and Franklin stay together. Their marriage changes. They are partners, not lovers.

Eleanor finds out about Franklin's **affair** in 1918.

These activists want women to win the vote.

Eleanor Becomes an Activist

Eleanor changes too. She wants to be more than a wife. She wants to be more than a mother. Eleanor wants to work outside her home. She becomes an activist. She wants to make life better for others.

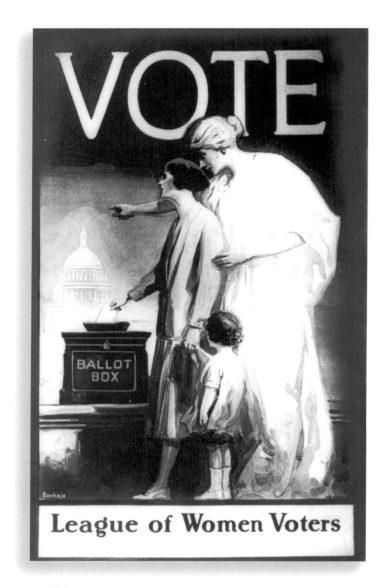

This poster shows a woman voting.

Eleanor Becomes an Activist

It is 1920. Women in the U.S. win the right to vote. Women have more power. Women become more active in politics. Eleanor becomes more active too. She works for women's groups. She makes friends with women who are activists.

Women's votes help bring social change.

Eleanor talks to some school children.

Eleanor's Beliefs

Eleanor has strong beliefs. She believes in **civil rights**. She believes in women's rights. She believes in workers' rights. She believes people need a good education. Eleanor believes libraries are important. She works hard for her beliefs.

Eleanor speaks on the radio in the early 1930s.

Eleanor's Beliefs

Eleanor begins to speak about her beliefs. At first, she is afraid of public speaking. In time, she gets over her fear. She becomes well known. She speaks on the radio. She writes for the newspaper.

"You must do the things you think you cannot do."

– *Eleanor Roosevelt*

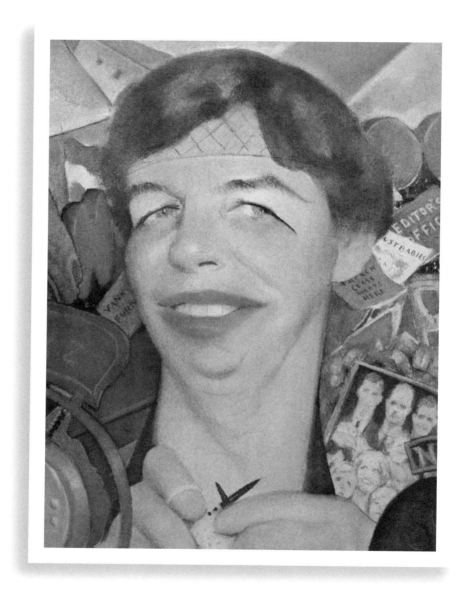

A 1933 cartoon of Eleanor Roosevelt.

Eleanor's Beliefs

Many people agree with Eleanor's beliefs. Others do not. Some call her "The **Gab**." Some people think she should stay home and knit. Eleanor says, "People must live their own life in their own way." Eleanor keeps working for her beliefs.

This mother and child are homeless.
1939

Eleanor's Work

By 1933, Franklin is U.S. President. The world is in a bad way. The **Great Depression** gets worse. About 15 million people cannot find work in the U.S. Many people are homeless and hungry. Eleanor supports programs to help women and youth.

The Great Depression lasts from 1929 to 1939.

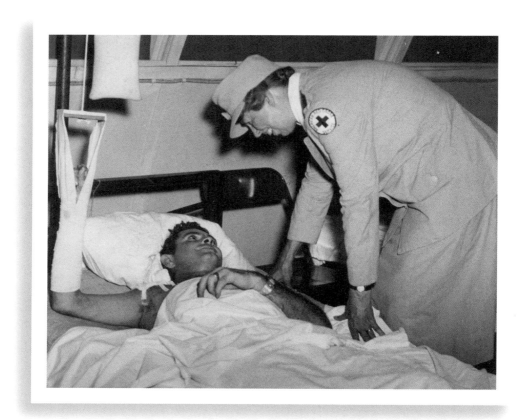

Eleanor visits a soldier in the hospital.

Eleanor's Work

World War II starts in 1939. Eleanor works for the Red Cross. She visits the U.S. troops. Franklin dies just before the war ends. Eleanor's 40 years with Franklin are over. Eleanor is on her own. She is 60 years old.

Franklin dies on April 12, 1945.

Eleanor and Winston Churchill stand beside Franklin's grave.

Eleanor holds the U.N. Declaration on Human Rights.

Eleanor's Work

Eleanor keeps doing good works. She works for civil rights in the U.S. Eleanor works for human rights in the United Nations. She travels the world to help others. Eleanor does her work with a "smile that never tires."

Eleanor writes 13 books after Franklin's death.

Eleanor Roosevelt

1844 – 1962

A Woman to Remember

November 7, 1962 is a sad day for the world. The White House flag flies at half-mast. Eleanor, first lady to the world, is dead. Eleanor laid a path for others to follow. Eleanor's work has made the world a better place.

Glossary

affair: a relationship between two people.

civil rights: equal rights for all people.

coming-out: young women meet bachelors from high society at a special dance.

gab: talk about things that are not important.

Great Depression: a time of high unemployment, falling stock prices, and low wages.

high society: upper class.

immigrant: a person who comes to a country to live there.

slum: a very poor and crowded place where people live.

White House: the U.S. President's home.

Talking About the Book

What did you learn about Eleanor Roosevelt?

What words would you use to describe Eleanor?

What losses did Eleanor experience in her life?

Do you think Eleanor was a feminist? Why or why not?

Eleanor says: "You must do the things you think you cannot do." Do you agree with Eleanor? Why or why not?

How did Eleanor made the U.S. a better place to live?

Picture Credits